GA
AND 1

More puns, one-liners and dad jokes

Written by Nick Jones
Edited by Ben Corrigan
Illustrations by Tiffany Sheely

Published by Full Media Ltd 2015

ISBN: 978-0-9930794-1-2

ABOUT THE AUTHOR

A proofreader and copywriter by trade, Nick Jones spends a lot of time working with words. But all work and no wordplay would make Nick a dull boy, so to redress the balance, Nick likes to write jokes in his spare time.

He published his first book, the Amazon bestseller *Gagged and Bound*, in 2014. Now he returns with *Gagged and Bound 2*, another collection of homemade puns, one-liners and dad jokes, accompanied by more hilarious illustrations by US artist Tiffany Sheely.

Nick lives in Cheshire, UK, with his wife, son and three cats.

INTRODUCTION

I started writing my first book, *Gagged and Bound*, in April 2014, and here I am in April 2015 writing the introduction for *Gagged and Bound 2*. What can I say about the last 12 months other than it's been a real roller-coaster year. The book didn't sell so I've been working as a ride operator at Thorpe Park ever since.

That was a joke, of course. But it has been an interesting year for me – *Gagged and Bound* has been a frequent Amazon bestseller in its category and enjoyed positive reviews from both the public and critics alike. Thanks to everyone who bought it and said nice things about it – you're one of the reasons I decided to write a sequel!

When you self-publish your first book, there's a lot of uncertainty involved. My first question was, 'How will it be received?' Then someone explained to me that self-published books are delivered by post, so that answered that. I'd like to thank all the postmen who have delivered copies of my book around the world.

Thanks to the *Gagged and Bound* team for working with me again for this sequel. Thanks to Ben Corrigan, whose meticulous editing skills, expert advice and words of encouragement have been invaluable, and to my proofreader Marion Adams for casting an eagle eye over the book. Thanks to my brother Richard for enduring my endless jokes via text and providing useful feedback. Thanks to Tiffany Sheely, my transatlantic illustrator, for designing the perfect cover and providing some wonderful cartoons, and to my good friend Chris Curley for designing the logo.

Finally, I wish to thank Ben and Richard along with my friends Dave Collingwood, Robin Allender, Hilary Cooksley, Jim Murphy and Daro Clark for kindly donating a joke or two. Keep them coming – this is going to be a trilogy!

DADICATION

This book is dedicated to my dad, whose jokes are so dad they're good.

GAGGED AND BOUND 2

I've got a pair of trousers that were handed down to me by my father, and by his father before him, and by his father before him. I'm not going to pass them on to my son, though – they're on their last legs now.

Why did the CEO make his staff wear roller blades? He wanted the company to run smoothly.

I cloned myself this morning and everything has gone wrong since. I guess I'm just having two of those days.

How much marijuana did the town crier buy? Announce.

In Texas, over 70% of people cheat on their partners, and 50% of them regret it. It's a sorry state of affairs.

I was in a clothes shop with my son, who needed some new shorts. He tried on some yellowy green ones and said, 'Dad! Look at these! Don't I look great?' I said, 'Son, don't get khaki.'

What did Pac-Man do after his successful ransom attempt? He gave up the ghost.

I left a dark grey Post-it on the fridge for my wife with the words, 'I've left you.' On a lighter note, I wrote, 'I'm only joking.'

I just read a book of 'A man goes into a bar'

gags. I didn't find it funny at all – it was full of inn jokes.

Why don't attractive Spanish people use umbrellas? Because the rain in Spain falls mainly on the plain.

My friend rushed up to me, shouting, '100 metres in 9.2 seconds! 100 metres in 9.2 seconds! 100 metres in 9.2 seconds!' I said, 'You sound like a broken record.'

Bob: My son has just applied for a job at a leading food manufacturer.
Barry: Unilever?
Bob: No, he's just finished his A-levels.

My friend asked if I'd ever seen a Guy Pearce

film. I said, 'Yeah, my flatmate did it last night before he microwaved a ready meal.'

I went into my accountant's office today, only to discover that he's not qualified. I was in unchartered territory.

How does He-Man change his colour TV to black and white? By the power of greyscale.

I once tied a mouse to a balloon full of helium and it flew off. Straight up.

I saw *The Curious Case of Benjamin Button* last night. It was like watching paint get wet.

For my stag do, my friends and I all played

poker. The best man won.

My mother-in-law kept moaning to me because she couldn't email a large file, so I told her to zip it.

What's the wettest part of the alphabet? H to O.

I just finished playing snakes and ladders. I was at the top of my game.

Did you hear about the dyslexic swordsman? He was very good with his words.

I got a job cleaning Big Ben. I have to work around the clock.

My wife once put lipstick, eyeliner and blusher on me. I was made up.

How to annoy PC World staff: spend hours on the internet on one of their computers, and when they ask you if you need assistance, say, 'No, thanks. I'm just browsing.'

I provide speech therapy for stammerers. I get lots of repeat business.

What's the secret to oriental comedy? Thai Ming.

I planned a trip to Belgium, the Netherlands and Luxembourg this year, but I had to cancel it at the last minute. Oh well, Benelux next time.

Dicing with death.

Teacher: Who can use the word 'ambiguous' in a sentence?

Pupil: I can, sir: 'I ambiguous small.'

Did you hear about the talented young footballer made of twigs? He soon got snapped up.

I bought some new scissors but they were so blunt I threw them out. They didn't make the cut.

There was a story on the news about a novel that has been printed with faulty ink that becomes soluble in certain conditions. The news reporter said, 'This story is expected to run and run.'

My sister can't stop purchasing white cuddly bears. She's got buy-polar disorder.

Bob: My nickname for my car is Oomph.
Barry: Because it's really fast?
Bob: No, that's the top speed.

Why are pet rabbits skint all the time? Because they're always getting cleaned out.

My 95-year-old aunt is no shrinking Violet. She's a shrinking Ethel.

Why did the collie dog get arrested in Mexico? Because it was a border cross.

My wife sent me to the shop to get some hair

lacquer. She was livid when I came home with Duncan Goodhew.

I've started a charity fund to help raise money for my obese cat. I'm having trouble getting it off the ground.

The most important part of the human body is the natal cleft. That's the bottom line.

I've got hundreds of artefacts. For instance, did you know that Van Gogh only had one ear?

Did you hear about the student who interrupted a law class by stripping naked? He wanted to pervert the course of justice.

If you go to the beach and, at the shoreline, get down on all fours, cover your left ear and put your right ear close to the sea, you can hear the inside of a shell.

Which is your favourite:
a) The sun
b) The moon
c) The stars
d) All of the above?

I'm raising money for my local hospital so they can buy high-quality bandages. It's for a good gauze.

Did you hear about the dishonest ventriloquist? He lied through his teeth.

I once had a panic attack while looking at the view from the top of the Eiffel Tower. It was breathtaking.

A chess champion was unfazed when his opponent keeled over and died mid-match. 'It's not the first time I've faced stiff competition,' he said.

Today was my first day in my new job tarmacking roads. We covered a lot of ground.

You should have seen the mad rush when they opened a new surgery for penis reductions. Men were falling over themselves.

Pete's a hut.

I've come up with my own version of *Stand By Me*. I put the TV on stand by and stare at my reflection.

When is it unwise to swallow your pride? When you're a lion.

Bob: I watched a band play in South East Asia last week.

Barry: Singapore?

Bob: No, he was pretty good actually.

My job is all about ticking boxes. I'm a bomb-disposal engineer.

Bob: I have a pet parrot that has free roam of my house, but I keep my wife in a cage.

Barry: Blimey, what does that say about you?

Bob: Nothing, I haven't taught it any words yet.

There was a hold-up at my local bank earlier. An old lady couldn't find her paying-in book.

My little boy is very musical. Yesterday when he was in the garden he made a bee flat.

What do a narrator and a male swinger have in common? They both like it in the third person.

Did you hear about the company that invented soluble aspirins? They dissolved.

Kermit the frog. What a Muppet.

I like to watch my daughter lying in her bed until she drops off. Is that cruel?

Bob: I just bought 10kg of snacks. Barry: Wow, that must have cost a bit! Bob: Nah, it was peanuts.

What did the heart say when it was tricked by the abdomen? 'Why aorta!'

Stevie Wonder. He's a key player in the music industry.

Why did the journalist break into an ice-cream van? He was looking for the inside scoop.

A chocoholic died after getting stuck in a store

room full of drink sachets. Eventually he ran out of Options.

Why did the man paint his van bright pink? He wanted a camper van.

Bob: Do you know what existed before the Big Bang?
Barry: No, I don't.
Bob: No matter.

I made a comment to a witch about her hat. It was rather pointed.

You have to be careful when talking to people from Yorkshire, as they don't pronounce their Hs. I asked a girl from Leeds to draw a figure of eight and she did a picture of Tony Blair.

Even at primary school I was obsessed with science. One time I overheard the other kids talking about the Fat Controller, and I thought they were referring to the pancreas and biliary system.

Patient: Doctor, I feel like a message in a fortune cookie.
Doctor: Don't worry; you'll snap out of it.

I'm taking part in a competition next week to see who can build the best rifle/knife combination. You've got to bayonet to win it.

I used to secretly wear my wife's satin gloves around the house when she was out, until she came home early one day and caught me red-handed.

The publishers of *Chrysanthemums Monthly* have made the controversial move of dedicating an edition to roses. It's a thorny issue.

Bob: This deck of playing cards is a bit tatty.
Barry: Deal with it.

I've just been to the local sheepdog trials. They were found guilty of seven counts of lamb slaughter.

What did the ceramic pot say to the Fugees? Kiln me softly.

Sudoku. It's a numbers game.

Thomas Edison works out how to create a long-lasting incandescent lamp using a carbon filament.

My friend bet me a tenner that he could beat me in a race. I'm going to give him a run for his money.

What do cannibals like on their toast? Middle-aged spread.

Bob: Guess what I just backed up on my drive?
Barry: I don't know, your holiday photos?
Bob: No, my new car.

Whenever I meet celebrity chefs, I get them to write their autograph on a special bowl. It's my signature dish.

Patient: Doctor, I seem to have telepathic powers.
Doctor: That's ridiculous! However, I am

impressed that you can speak without moving your lips.

This girl came up to me and said, 'You look like a small glass of ouzo.' I thought, *That's a cheap shot.*

My friend put a speck of dust on my arm as a practical joke. It was lost on me.

I was born in the mid-seventies. It was 75 degrees Fahrenheit in the labour ward.

The trouble with John Lennon was that he often saw the world through rose-tinted specs.

I went to a used-car dealer and said I wanted

to buy the flashiest, most expensive car he had, but he just gave me the run-around.

A friend has asked me to film his wedding, but the zoom button has broken on my camera. I'm not sure how it's going to pan out.

I've released a single about batteries. It's a double A-side.

When it comes to meal times, I find that breakfast, lunch, dinner and supper is the order of the day.

I told my friend a joke on the phone and she said she was grinning from ear to ear. I said, 'You're grinning from where to where?'

Patient: Doctor, I'm confused about my diagnosis.

Doctor: OK, let me give you an analogy.

Patient: Please don't – I already suffer from hay fever.

I'm hosting a dinner party in an hour's time, and I've just realised my carving knife is blunt. I need to get a new one, sharpish.

My friend's always catching fire. He's a juggler.

A new study claims that men who purchase the household shopping are better in bed. I don't buy it.

I had a new three-piece fitted by my tailor

while skydiving. Suited me down to the ground.

My brother was very supportive when I played the role of a pantomime horse. In fact, he was behind me all the way.

Never forget your roots. That's what my wife's hairdresser always says to her.

I just attached feet to the legs of my computer desk. I'm not going to take them off again because that would de-feet the object.

I'm doing two Open University courses at the moment. I signed up to do French and the rest is History.

PEOPLE WHO WRITE LIKE THIS DESERVE CAPITAL PUNISHMENT.

Patient: Doctor, I can't stop self-harming.
Doctor: Don't beat yourself up about it.

I just found out how the other half lives. Apparently, she's sleeping with her gym instructor and wants a divorce.

Did you hear about the fight that broke out on a moving stairway? That escalated quickly.

I tried working as a shepherd once, but I couldn't find a shop that sold crooks. You just can't get the staff these days.

Stonehenge rocks.

Bob: A friend of mine died last week. He was buried alive under some sort of concrete.
Barry: Was it asphalt?
Bob: No, it was his wife's fault.

I used to be a font designer. That was character building.

Did you hear about the guy who stuck wings on his car? It flew through its MOT.

I once gave a dinner-party guest a glass of wine with a wasp in it. That didn't go down well.

How did the somnambulist climb Everest? She slept her way to the top.

Did you hear about the factory worker who died rescuing his colleague from a vat of chickpea dip? He was given a post-hummus award.

Comfort eating is really bad for you. In fact, consuming any brand of fabric conditioner is going to be harmful.

What does David Blaine do when people call him a fake in the street? He rises above it.

Bob: My grandson was named after me. Barry: Well, he wouldn't have been named before you, would he?

If you taste vomit or stomach acid when you burp, you're sick in the head.

I love my lungs. They're very close to my heart.

Premature Ejaculation – The Movie. Coming soon.

I accidentally fired an overweight male hen out of a cannon. It was just one big cock up.

I had a wardrobe malfunction today. The door fell off.

Did you hear about the suicidal man who went on holiday to Barry Island? It was his last resort.

I don't let my son listen to UK garage music. It

keeps him off The Streets.

Bob: I recently got divorced. We agreed that we both wanted different things.

Barry: It was amicable, then?

Bob: No. I wanted to stay together, and she wanted a divorce.

A whistleblower has come forward to reveal that the world of football refereeing is corrupt.

It was my wife's birthday yesterday, so I decided that I would do absolutely nothing. It was the least I could do.

A local bicycle manufacturer is in trouble for selling bikes with faulty brakes. The company's spokesperson said, 'Don't blame me – blame the brakes person.'

Why do boxers hold their gloves up when attacked? To save face.

I went to the doctor about a red patch on my arm. He took one quick look and said, 'That's dermatitis' – it was a rash decision.

My wife's always going out on the pull. She's in a tug-of-war team.

You know who I find really pig-headed? Pigs.

The world's tallest man is starring as one of the seven dwarves in *Snow White*. Critics have described his performance as unmissable.

Sex addicts, swingers and doggers … they're all bonkers.

Don't you hate it when you're in your car and someone doesn't bother flashing when you let them out? Normally they just say 'Goodbye' and walk off.

The only time I have German white wine is as an ingredient in a meal. I have it on an add-hock basis.

I'm under a lot of pressure in my job. I'm a scuba-diving instructor.

It's best not to have any skeletons in your closet. Under the patio is a better option.

I went into an antique shop today. Nothing new there.

Did you hear about the thief who stole a load of dictionaries? He's got away with words.

Bob: My wife was banging on earlier about how much she loves the little rabbit in *Bambi*.
Barry: Thumper?
Bob: No, I just told her to shut up.

Have you heard that new band, Paranoid? Everyone's talking about them.

Why does Miley Cyrus have a car? To get twerk.

Apparently, Charles Windsor is a talented watercolourist. He's the artist formally known as Prince.

How do PR professionals operate an ejector seat? They press release.

When I got married, my wife made me sign a prenup. I found it really difficult, but luckily my wife was really helpful. She said, 'Leave everything to me.'

I bought a new stereo for my car. It's bigger than the old one; in fact, it's double-DIN size.

I was staying in this hotel, and in the morning the door opened and a staff member chucked a plate of food across the room. Sausages, egg,

43

bacon, mushrooms and beans flew everywhere! It was a right mess. I rang reception and asked what the hell was going on, and the receptionist said, 'We told you when you booked that we'd throw in a free breakfast.'

December 24th is Christmas and December 31st is New Year's. Sorry – sometimes I can't help Eves dropping.

I went to a presentation about drilling holes. Talk about boring.

What does the McDonald's CEO have in common with a lion? They're both at the top of the food chain.

Whenever I read a book, I always forget which page I've reached, but today I turned a corner.

Why did the schoolboy cover himself in Christmas lights before sitting his GCSEs? Because he wanted to shine in his exams.

I once tried smuggling drugs through airport customs. I really stuffed it up.

Bob: My mate says he's slept with over a thousand women. What do you reckon he's got that we haven't?
Barry: Herpes, probably.

I saw a pigeon helping a sparrow build a new nest. It was a re-homing pigeon.

Jeremy Klaxon.

I've got fifty shades of grey on my Kindle. I think the screen's broken.

Me and my friend like to have conversations in reverse. It always ends on a 'Hi'.

I saw *Schindler's List* in 3D last night. That really put things into perspective.

My next book is going to be aimed at racists. It'll be a hardback and I'll throw it at them in the street.

Bob: I just overheard someone saying that I smell.

Barry: Sounds like you just got wind.

I got expelled from school after my first ever class. That teacher taught me a lesson.

I saw a policewoman wandering round with a taser. She was stunning.

I put my laptop in flight mode, threw it out of a window and it dropped straight onto the road and smashed into pieces.

My son's at the age where he asks 'Why?' all the time. Things like, 'Why did you leave us?', 'Why have you changed your name?' and 'Why won't you open the door when I know you're in there, you bastard?'

My new year's resolution was to stop exaggerating. Best thing I ever did.

I was walking down a street in Mumbai when I saw a man eating tiger. I asked him, 'Why on earth would you want to eat a tiger?'

My dad's always bending the rules, which is why he lost his job at the stationer's.

I've just finished proofreading a novel about werewolves. There were lots of howlers in it.

My exercise routine consists of doing a hundred press-ups every night. I press 'up' on my PlayStation controller a hundred times.

The Society of Viagra Users just gave my grandfather an award for longest-standing member.

What was Steve Jobs' favourite dessert? Apple turnover.

My mate always carries a video camera when he watches a magic show. He never misses a trick.

I'm so excited! I've just paid a sculptor to make a bust of me! Sorry, I'm getting a head of myself.

Clowns are so ungrateful. I once offered one a custard pie and he threw it right back in my face.

When a woman is asked how she likes her men, she always thinks long and hard before answering.

A couple are sat in their kitchen one morning when their pet tomcat comes home wearing make-up, high heels and a long blonde wig. The man looks at his pet and then turns to his wife and says, 'Hey, love, look what the cat dragged in.'

I went to pick my son up after work and when I got home I realised I had someone else's son in the back of the car. Schoolboy error.

I'm on a ferry with my family but there's nothing to do. All are bored!

Did you know they make Viagra for women as well now? What's up with that?

I met John Cleese once. I said to him excitedly,

'Thanks so much for *Fawlty Towers*, it was so funny, especially the one about the war.' He said, 'Don't mention it.'

Someone just compared my music to two famous composers. It was a Bach-Handel compliment.

I am going to an event later today for start-up companies. It's being held at Brands Hatch.

I arranged a day for an estate agent to come and value my house. When he turned up, he forced his way into the house, knocked me to the floor and tied my hands and feet together. As he pulled a whip out and started brandishing it, I screamed, 'What the hell are you doing?' He replied, 'Well, when I emailed you to confirm the appointment, you sent one back asking me to give you a rough time.'

There's a huge survey taking place in our town but loads of people are refusing to turn up. The local council are hoping everyone comes to their census.

When people ask me how old I am, I give them an approximate age. I like people to know what I'm about.

I saw a cockney eating some stairs earlier.

I quite like Bruce Willis action movies, but I wouldn't say I'm a die-hard fan.

With books you get words, with CDs you get sound, with TV ... well, you get the picture.

French businesses. They go the extra kilometre.

Since I started dressing as a ninja and my wife started wearing a burka, we don't really see much of each other.

When alcohol comes into contact with carpet, it can be very costly. Once I accidentally dropped a free carpet sample into a glass of expensive wine – what a waste!

I just bought a complete set of encyclopedias in audiobook format. That speaks volumes.

Lance Armstrong. He just can't compete.

I once had a snowboard taster session. It tasted horrible.

This guy came up to me in the street and said, 'Do you know where the post office is?' I said, 'No.' He said, 'It's down that road on the left.'

Why do brides' dresses reach the floor? So they don't get cold feet.

My motto is 'Look out for number one'. I work in an incontinence ward.

Why did the movie *Kleptomania* take so long to film? Because every scene required a lot of takes.

My wife gave me the silent treatment yesterday. My ears were blocked and she put some drops in for me.

The first thing I did after that was listen to the radio. It was music to my ears.

My friends and I like to sit in a circle and hand a clock round. It's a good way to pass the time.

Is it just me, or do people seem to ask a lot of paranoid, self-doubting questions these days?

I was in a restaurant with my wife when this huge guy interrupted our meal and aggressively asked me where the toilets were. I told him where to go.

If Jesus came back, imagine how many followers he'd have on Twitter.

Every week I buy the same ten items from the pound shop, and I pay for them with a tenner. No change there.

All the cemeteries in our town are full. It's giving the council grave concerns.

At the zoo I saw a large female cat let a group of male cats mate with her one after the other. I thought: *Whoa – easy tiger*.

Shaving Cream.

My grandfather was a river enthusiast, and every year he'd go to Paris for his holiday. We'd then have to sit through a slideshow of his holiday photos. It was just more of the Seine.

I went to the barber's for a short back and sides, but all he did was take one small chunk of hair out of the fringe. I thought, *That's a bit off.*

I need to dye my hair blonde, to be fair.

There were reports recently of an alien sighting on a farm in Wiltshire. The press had a field day.

I took my wife for a special meal yesterday at

Royal Ascot. It's a bit different because you get to ride a horse round a track for an hour, then you have a meal consisting of a starter, salad, main course and dessert. My wife didn't enjoy the experience, but I loved it. It's horses, four courses.

I just watched that new film *Paralysed*. I wasn't feeling it.

If the person who invented the piggy bank had patented it, it could have become a cash cow.

Did you hear about the time Captain Hook got attacked by a mob? He beat them up singlehandedly.

When I was a kid, we had to be in school from

9 to 5. Now they just go in from 8 till 3:30. How times have changed.

Patient: Doctor, I want to jack my job in and go and work in a labour ward.

Doctor: Sounds like you're having a midwife crisis.

I just got fired by a leading clothing retailer for having a bad attitude. Whatever, Next!

Have you heard the joke about Dorian Gray? Never gets old.

When people say they watch a TV programme on and off, how do they do that exactly?

A man was due in court today for stealing an invisibility cloak. He didn't show up.

What antivirus software does Luis Suárez use? Bitdefender.

My most treasured possession is my sat nav. I'd be lost without it.

Patient: Doctor, I think I've died and become a ghost. Doctor?

Did you hear about the caterpillar that opened its own library? It advertised using the slogan, 'Take a book out of my leaf.'

I did an art piece at the Tate recently which

involved me being fired out of a cannon through a brick wall. I won an award for best breakthrough artist.

Bob: I'm thinking of creating one of those mind-maps.
Barry: Have you lost your mind?

I was suspended from school once. The teacher was so annoyed with me that he dangled me out of a window by my tie.

Have you seen that new TV show where the presenters go round humiliating policemen? It's called *Embarrassing Bobbies*.

I once wasted a whole day reading about Minotaurs, Jason and the Argonauts, and

Icarus. I felt pretty mythed after that.

Jim Morrison's voice isn't great on his first record, but I guess it's early Doors.

What happened when two students raced each other to hand their coursework in? One was beaten to submission.

I thought I was a goner once. It turned out I was just a dyslexic Arsenal fan.

Ronnie Corbett went to audition for the role of Darth Vader in *Star Wars*, but he turned up an hour after he was meant to. Too little, too late.

Do you know what really gives me grief?

Reading the obituaries.

Everything I do in my job is counter-productive. I work for a checkout manufacturer.

How does a new car feel when it's driven off the forecourt? Used.

I don't think I'll ever figure out how to measure an object's heaviness. No weigh know-how.

In a recent interview, Nick Berry said that if the chance arose to stage a TV comeback, he'd return in a *Heartbeat*.

Ken Dodd once walked past me with his feather duster and gently brushed my elbow. That tickled my funny bone.

How do you confuse a Premiership goalkeeper? Ask him, 'What's your net worth?'

I was pulled over by a cop wearing sunglasses. He'd taken a very dim view of my driving.

My wife put me in an awkward position earlier. She's a judo expert.

I've got a two-legged chair at home. I can't stand it.

Bob: I want to go on one of those online

discussion sites to voice my opinions about speed cameras.

Barry: Forum?

Bob: No, I'm against 'em.

Don Johnson was prosecuted for stealing pig carcasses from a butcher's. When asked in court to explain his actions, he said, 'It's my hammy vice.'

A snail race has dominated the headlines in our town today. It was a slow news day.

My wife kept making me watch American TV serials so eventually I told her to get lost. Big mistake.

I went to a car showroom wearing a high-vis

jacket. They saw me coming.

Snoop Dogg and Dr Dre have broken the world record for rolling the longest spliff. It was a joint effort.

I once asked a deaf smoker to lend me an ashtray and she led me astray.

Did you hear about the office manager who got sacked for his interview style? He thought it would relax the candidates if he stripped off naked.

I had to pick up Larry David from the airport, so I went to arrivals and held a placard with his name on it. Unfortunately the sign failed.

Nobody was surprised when *Rain Man* won Oscars for Best Picture, Best Original Screenplay, Best Director and Best Actor in a Leading Role. It was a four-gong conclusion.

I was playing with my son when this guy looked at me funny, so I rearranged his face. We were having a game of Mr Potato Head.

My auntie went to Boots and asked for a vajazzle. She meant Vagisil.

Bob: Have you ever made love in front of a fireplace?
Barry: You know me; I don't do things by hearths.

Did you hear about the street performer who

trained his dog to balance revolving coins on its nose? It was a good money-spinner.

A friend of mine was killed by a superbug the other day. Poor guy, eaten alive by a 20ft spider.

Did you know that Brian Eno has a brother from Manila called Phillip?

Bob: Did mammoths have any close genetic relatives?
Barry: They mastodon.

How did Sherlock Holmes do his tax return? Using the power of deduction.

A new product has taken Scottish chip shops by storm. It's called I Can't Believe It's Not Batter.

Elvis adored succulent chicken. That's why he used to sing, 'Love meat tender'.

The other night I was so miserable I didn't sleep a wink. I was tossing and turning until eventually my wife turned the light on and said, 'Someone's got into bed on the wrong side tonight.'

The earth wires played the live wires in a football match. It was a great game for the neutrals.

Where do Afghans go to buy their

mayonnaise? Hellman's Province.

Wanted: trainee human cannonballs. Successful candidates will need to be fired up.

Tommy Lee Jones and Will Smith are starring in a new film where they try to rid the world of a deadly virus. It's called *Men In Gitis*.

I met up with some friends recently, and one of them had put on a huge amount of weight. We managed to have a good chat without mentioning the elephant in the room.

I just upgraded my 32-bit computer to 64-bit. Using a sledgehammer.

Did you hear about the old man who bought some Viagra and a treadmill? He was up and running in no time.

I just read about a foundry that's producing bronzes of former Royal Family members. Apparently the Di has been cast.

I had a terrifying experience with a carving knife when I was younger. Scarred me for life.

A new ultra-violent version of Edward Woodward's classic 1980s TV show is being released. It's called *The Graphic Equalizer*.

I got a new TV for Christmas. My new year's resolution: 1080p.

A woman had a go at her husband for never being spontaneous, so he burst into flames right there in his armchair.

What did Archimedes say whenever someone farted? 'You reek! Ugh!'

I was watching American football while drinking a glass of milk when all of a sudden I came out in spots. Turns out it was NFL-lactic shock.

My secretary giggles every time she writes a note in meetings. She's a laugh a minute.

For Christmas I bought each of my relatives a mannequin leg. It's the perfect stocking filler.

I set up a telephone canvassing company once but it went bust. Apparently nobody wants their phone covered in tarpaulin.

Who sang *Mysterious Girl* and got eaten before a main course? Peter Entrée.

I asked my wife to buy me a pencil, but when she gave it to me I was disappointed. I wanted one of medium hardness, but sadly it wasn't 2B.

I just saw a woman with the perfect bum. Hind sight is a wonderful thing.

I'm able to spot cream puffs out the corner of my eye. I just use my profiterole vision.

Did you hear about the anti-rolling-tobacco campaign that backfired spectacularly? The slogan was 'Pack it in.'

I just saw one of Britain's best-loved actors dressed as Santa. It was a Blessed in disguise.

Hasbro are planning to stop selling Monopoly. When asked why, they said, 'Because there's no real money in it.'

What do you call a group of wolves who are shedding their fur? A moulty pack.

A chef just set a new world record for making the deepest pizza base, which is 20 metres tall. That'll be hard to top.

My dad had his nostril hair removed using electrolysis. The results were great, but they charged him through the nose.

Bob: I'm always lighting matches.

Barry: Are you a pyromaniac?

Bob: No, I'm a floodlight manufacturer.

I just saw a load of birds fighting over a dead carcass. What a carrion.

Teacher: What's an umbrella term?

Pupil: Autumn?

I went to a fair recently, but due to a lack of money I decided not to visit the clairvoyant. That cost me a fortune.

Bob: Are you coming Morris dancing tomorrow?

Barry: Yeah, I'll be there with bells on.

I won a competition to spend a day with a famous Hollywood couple, but when I arrived at their mansion they weren't there. It was the Pitts'.

Does your daughter need any new doors? I can help; I'm a daughter door salesman.

I go to a maths club. Every week we get together and work out a load of equations, and then sum.

Robert Langdon. He's in Dan Brown's bad books.

Punch drunk.

Bob: I've just read *1984*.

Barry: That's Orwell and good.

A struggling toilet-tissue manufacturer plans to launch a new toilet roll to turn its fortunes around. If you ask me, it's just paper over the cracks.

How do trees feel in spring? Releaved.

Did you hear about the man who tried inhaling nitrous oxide while slicing an onion? He didn't know whether to laugh or cry.

Colostomy bags. They really take it out of you.

Bob: Would you say you're indecisive?

Barry: Yes and no.

As I was driving my car through fog the other day, I started wondering what causes fog to form in the first place. Suddenly it all became clear.

Rulers. They're made to measure.

Back in the 1970s, I met the Village People in a bar, and they were going on and on about how fun it is to stay at the YMCA. I said, 'OK! Don't make a song and dance about it.'

This woman just had a go at me for trying to get into her knickers. I told her it was her fault for leaving them lying on the beach.

Wall: What a weekend! I got plastered on Saturday, and then I got hammered on Sunday.

Picture: Well I'm hanging today.

Did you hear about the guy who went out with a blow-up doll? When he dumped her, he made sure he let her down gently.

My friend was worried about whether she should let her young daughter have a mobile. I couldn't understand it: it's just bits of plastic dangling from string above her cot.

Did you hear about the Eskimo whose mouth kept freezing shut? The doctor told him to grit his teeth and bear it.

Incest. It's a family affair.

Bob: I've got this mate who talks like he's swallowed a dictionary.

Barry: You mean he uses a lot of long words?

Bob: No, he points at his throat and grunts.

I watched a film about a submarine last night. It was deeply moving.

A policeman caught me painting a counterfeit Mona Lisa. I said to him, 'It's not what it looks like.'

I went through a phase of watching what I was eating, but my wife said it made me look cross-eyed.

A souvenir shop in the Russian capital is having a closing-down sale. Everything Moscow.

Did you hear about the rich loner who bought a town in Wiltshire? He was left to his own Devizes.

How often does a Smurf get its bum out? Once in a blue moon.

I'm very modest. I hate mods.

I got arrested for attempted theft in the Tate Museum last week. When questioned, I explained that their website states that pictures can be taken in the main gallery for personal, non-commercial use.

85

Bob: I've come up with an alternative to counting sheep that is going to take the world by storm!

Barry: Don't count your chickens.

I am a huge fan of Wikipedia. Does that make me a Wikipedophile?

My wife got so sick of me going fishing all the time that she said one day, 'If you don't quit fishing right now, I'm going to leave you.' That sent me reeling.

Did you hear about the man who fell out of a plane and landed in hay? He was saved by the bale.

I've started adding my favourite herb to tea.

It's a thyme-consuming activity.

One of America's most famous singers has gone on tour with her doppelgänger. Their act is called Cher and Cheralike.

Patient: Doctor, what's the best way of getting rid of earache?
Doctor: Get a divorce.

I wore my shoes out today. It seemed pointless keeping them in the house all the time.

City Link have just gone into administration. I reckon they'd be better off sticking to delivering parcels.

The tables have turned.

I was bursting for the loo while hiking in the countryside, so I decided to urinate in a wheat field. Talk about going against the grain.

My favourite animal is the jellyfish. It's a no-brainer.

I surprised my wife today by buying her a new pair of high heels. I like to keep her on her toes.

Bob: I can't think of the word for a cascade of water falling from a height.
Barry: What a fool.
Bob: That's the one.

China's pet-food industry is so competitive that one company's started using controversial ingredients. It's dog eat dog.

I always thought dinosaurs looked fat when I saw them in films, but then I went to the Natural History Museum. Turns out they were just big-boned.

I just watched the FA Cup Final while suffering from severe diarrhoea. It was end-to-end stuff.

Why do U2 always win celebrity tennis matches? Because they have a competitive Edge.

I've spent so long reading books about Greek gods that I don't know what deities.

I camped outside the Apple store one winter's night just to get the brand new iPad. It was worth its wait in cold.

When the chips are down, it's usually time to buy a new computer.

I was drunk at a wedding reception when suddenly the bride and groom wheeled a bucking bronco onto the dancefloor. That really threw me.

I went to a dogs' home and asked for advice about getting a couple of dogs. They gave me some Pointers.

A woman was whinging to a colleague in IT about her sex life, saying how her husband always gets excited too quickly. Her colleague said, 'Have you tried turning him off and on again?'

Bob: I was in a car park earlier, and the level I parked on had a much higher ceiling than all the others.

Barry: Sounds like a tall storey.

I wandered into a Catholic church service and was condemned for my attire. I knew then that I'd reached critical mass.

Why was the camel arguing with the whale? He wanted his humpback.

I just read an article about the retired German footballer Wolfgang Wolf. That's a name and a half.

Some sage advice for job seekers: don't lie on your CV. Nobody will be able to read it.

A friend of mine made a wisecrack about the untidiness of my garage, but I didn't find it funny. It was too close to home.

I went into a computer store and asked to see a salesman, and the person I spoke to said, 'Sorry, sir, but the correct term these days is salesperson.' I'd forgotten I was in PC World.

There were ugly clashes between environmental activists and the police today. Green never goes well with blue.

It must be nerve-wracking being the recipient of mouth-to-mouth resuscitation – having someone breathing down your neck like that.

My wife and I both love those chocolate eggs with the toy inside. We're Kinder Egg spirits.

What do you get if you take *1999* and add the numbers from *Nothing Compares 2 U*, *17 Days*, *I Would Die 4 U* and *4 The Tears In Your Eyes*? A Princely sum.

Gone soft in your old age? Try Viagra.

A few years ago I announced that I was retraining to become a plastic surgeon. That led to a few raised eyebrows.

My boss is a hideous freak of nature, although

94

I know I shouldn't say that out loud. He has eyes and ears everywhere.

I was going to buy a corned beef and potato ready meal, but there was no price on it. #nohashtag.

A man came up to me and offered me a packet of herbs, but I noticed the packet was damaged. So he said, 'No problem,' and put some Sellotape around it. That sealed the dill.

If you experience the pot calling the kettle black, you've probably smoked too much pot.

My wife reminded me that it's our anniversary next week so I've made a mental note of it. It says, 'Flobbalobbywoobledeewoo.'

I find social media overwhelming, but I do think I finally have a handle on Twitter. It's @nickjonezy.

I took a nutrition course recently, which involved an exam at the end. The examiner seemed very stern. She said, 'You'll pass this if you know what's good for you.'

I opened the curtains this morning. Now I just need to put them up.

I just saw a wolf outside a little pig's house, huffing and puffing about something. Hopefully it'll blow over.

When you get off a plane, wait by the baggage carousel and everyone points and laughs at your tatty old luggage, that's the worst case scenario.

I can count the number of fingers I have on one hand on one hand.

What's the temperature like in a beehive? Swarm.

My dog is obese, so I've bought it a special mini-gym with weights and everything. I really hope it works out.

The best Olympic event involves a heavy round object: discus.

I spilt some orange juice on my violin. Fiddle

sticks!

Why did George Lucas crave chocolate? Because his Galaxy was far, far away.

I went for an interview at Clearasil yesterday. They offered me a job on the spot.

The reed pen was the pre-quill to the feather-based pen.

What happened when the shape-shifter was accused of committing crimes? He turned himself into the police.

I was chatting to a woman at a party about a book I was writing, and she said, 'Great! Can I write an introduction for you?' That's what I call foreword.

I wasn't that impressed with the *Shrek* films. I thought they were mediogre.

A new type of mobile phone has been designed for soldiers. It features 'Incoming!' calls.

I just finished assembling a 250-piece jigsaw. That'll teach me to buy power tools from IKEA.

A new passenger aircraft has been developed which bounces if it crash-lands. It's called a Boing 747.

I did a presentation to the National Society of Mutes. I'm sure I speak for everyone who attended when I say it went well.

I just read a novel about an immortal dog. Couldn't put it down.

A woman in the US is suing her cosmetic surgeon for shoddy work. There's a rumour that he has offered her free corrective surgery, but so far she has remained tight-lipped.

Barclaycard always let me know how much I owe them. Credit where it's due.

For a lot of people the UK horsemeat scandal of 2013 was a bit of a mare.

GAGGED AND BOUND 2

What do you get if you cross a cat with a serving dish? A platter puss.

I just listened to a song made up of samples of dogs breathing heavily. It was pants.

My children say I'm old and past it, but I'm still down with the kids. For instance, I've just bought one of those cell phones, or 'cellphies' as some people call them.

I hate these self-centred opera singers. It's just 'Mi mi mi …'

A goblin from Middle-earth just came up to me and said, 'Sharkû', but I had no idea what it meant. Orc word!

101

Rearrange these letters to form a word:

ENECIOVL

(Sometimes violence is the answer.)

What sort of travellers does a cannibal like? Seasoned ones.

Bob: I might go to Chişinău for my holiday.
Barry: Moldova?
Bob: Yeah, I've given it a lot of thought.

Apparently someone has stolen all the barrels from Courage. They have trouble brewing in that company.

I finally got round to watching *Back to the Future* last night. It's about time.

I went to the optician's for an eye test. He held up a load of letters and it was easy to see Y.

If you're planning a skiing trip in the Alps, don't go off-peak. That's way too high.

I lost my job as a care-home assistant. I couldn't care less.

I was describing my favourite Microsoft Office program to a rapper the other day. He nodded and said, 'Word'.

James Brown once asked me to show him the sights of Bristol. First I took him to Temple Meads Station, then I showed him the SS Great Britain, and finally we went to Bristol Zoo. After all that I asked him if there was anything else he wanted to see, and he said, 'Take me to the bridge!'

There was a special offer on at our local hairdresser's last week. Perms and conditions applied.

Old friends are like recliner chairs. They go back a long way.

I've written a book about an award-winning wine vault. It's a best cellar.

If you want to work in a fish and chip shop, you need to know your plaice.

I have this recurring nightmare where I'm being chased by an infinite number of 3s.

My favourite word is plethora. It means a lot.

I tried working as a shepherd once, but every time I counted the sheep I fell asleep.

Sony are using a new extra-strong material for all their mp3 players, hi-fis and other audio devices. Personally, I think it's wrong to reinforce stereo types.

Election riggers. They're just there to make up the numbers.

My local Chinese takeaway has started serving wildfowl, so I thought I'd have a gander.

If you know someone who's overly sensitive about their weight, don't tell them they need to lighten up.

I have this psychic friend who makes jokes about disasters before they happen. Too soon?

My friend said to me, 'In my local supermarket, a box of six medium free range is £1, while twelve medium free range is £1.90. Six large free range are £1.20, six organic free range are £1.50, and six large organic free range are £1.80.' I said, 'And what has that got to do with the price of eggs?'

I've been constipated for seven days now. I just can't work it out.

A terrorist cell in Ipswich have been arrested after a spate of murders in which they smothered their victims. Police have dubbed them the Suffolk Eight.

Time Will Tell.

I posted an incriminating photo of myself on Facebook which led to my arrest. I've only got my selfie to blame.

The UN doesn't stand for any nonsense. It stands for United Nations.

I don't like the trailers for the *Fast & Furious* movies. Too many spoilers.

Stephen Hawking. He has an answer for everything.

Every night I read a book in bed, and then I sleep on top of it. It's good for the spine.

I watched a movie about a pig. It had a twist at

the end.

Bob: What's this white thing? It's freezing!
Barry: It's a freezer.

I once edited the biography of a judge. He wasn't happy with my work at all. In fact, he threw the book at me.

Exit signs are the way to go.

I always have pressing issues in my job. I work for a magazine printing company.

Gambling rules are always changing for the better.

If you retweet something with a hashtag, is that a rehash?

My boss always says, 'Put yourself in your customer's shoes,' which is why he lost his previous job at Clarks.

I had a Chinese omelette earlier but I couldn't finish it. Too much fu yung.

After sustaining a head injury, I woke up thinking I was either the Southampton FC manager or a Nazi leader from the 1940s. I didn't know if I was Koeman or Göring.

My doorbell's broken. I'm worried about the knock-on effects.

Who are the most anal rock band in the world? OCDC.

I bought a parrot last week, which speaks for itself really.

What does a soldier shout the morning after a curry? 'Fire in the hole!'

Despite me pestering her repeatedly, my wife wouldn't let me try on her coat made from baby-bird feathers. I wore her down eventually.

You really need to aim for the stars if you want to become a world-famous assassin.

I go horse riding with my wife every weekend, although we don't get on with each other. It would be too heavy for the horse.

My mate's spilt treacle on his dog. That's a very sticky whippet.

After a string of failures, my son is hoping that his new conker will be a success.

Why do sodium chloride suppliers all hate each other? Because they always trade in salts.

I moved from Cornwall to London five years ago. Long time, no sea.

Bob: Have you seen that new TV show, *PMT*?

Barry: No. Is it a period drama?

I was hiking across the moors with a friend, and we reached some boggy marshland. As we traipsed through it, I said to my friend, 'It's trying terrain.' He looked up and said, 'No it isn't – it's a beautiful sunny day.'

The gingerbread man. He's an unsavoury character.

I've written a children's book about a dog playing in a garden. It's ruff around the hedges.

A new study claims that alcoholism can be cured by replacing drink with ecstasy. However, the test subjects are suing the researchers for leaving them high and dry.

My friend gave a customer a knuckle sandwich, which is why he was fired by Subway.

It's the national hairdressing championships today. The highlights will be on later.

People often insinuate that my sister is manly, but she doesn't mind. She's got broad shoulders.

Prisoners: they're all crying on the inside.

Jonathan Ross got in trouble when he told his wife he'd just been on *The Wright Stuff*.

Why is dial the most relaxed word in the English language? Because it's laid back.

Avoid walking down dark lanes. I went down one last night and got hit in the back of the leg by a ten-pin bowling ball.

Due to poor sales, a birdcage manufacturer is giving away its remaining stock to hamster owners. No perches necessary.

Bob: I'm thinking of adding a twin exhaust to my car.
Barry: Really? To what end?
Bob: To the back end.

I tried to write a message in Morse code just using dots, but in the end I had to dash.

I can't stand that way of serving potatoes mixed with wickets and stumps. It's just not croquette.

Why aren't Red Arrows pilots worried about tests? Because they always pass with flying colours.

I went to church on Sunday, and the vicar gave a sermon in which he talked about how Moses had died on the Cross and how Jesus had parted the seas. Afterwards I went up to him and said, 'You need to practise what you preach.'

My parents have spent a lot of time behind bars. They're retired publicans.

Exorcists. They scare the hell out of people.

My auntie bought me an odourless deodorant for Christmas. It didn't make any scents.

When I was a kid, I was being naughty one day, so my mum shouted, 'Just you wait till your father gets home!' But that was the day he ran off with another woman and we never saw him again, so I had the last laugh there.

Why was the rabbit on the news? Because its owner ran out of sawdust.

The first time we gave our son a bowl of icing and a wooden spoon, he went stir-crazy.

What would a proofreader do if someone crossed a football to him? Edit.

When I was a kid I stayed at a friend's house one night, and in the morning we found his dad lying on the kitchen floor asleep, with empty bottles of ketchup everywhere. My friend sighed and shouted, 'Mum! Dad's been on the sauce again!'

Last night, a bunch of men pinned me down in the street and dressed me as a black private detective. I was Shafted.

Why are footballers suspected of carrying drugs? Because they often get caught in possession.

I just fell in marshland and got some in my mouth. It's all gone peat tongue.

There's a special offer on at our local cinema to watch *Harry Potter*. It's only a quid each.

Did you hear about the lazy drug addict? It took him a while to get into gear.

My wife says I'm bad at describing people. I tell you, that woman is something else.

My boss has an open-door policy. If you don't open the door for him, he'll fire you.

Whenever I'm stressed out I like to boil the kettle. It's a good way to let off steam.

If I had a pound for every time someone said I was obsessed with money, I'd have £1,826.

I dreamt last night that I was eating a huge mound of rice, and when I woke up my pilau had gone.

I made a mountain out of a molehill earlier. It's a lot harder than people say it is.

I've opened a shop selling tall ships. Sails are through the roof.

Journalist: How important was the death of your singer to the sound of your last album?
Guitarist: It was instrumental.

Have you seen that website that encourages people to urinate by random vehicles? It's called WeeByAnyCar.com.

A friend of mine recently had to admit to his wife that he was gay. There was mounting evidence.

A dwarf walked into a bar. It was a tow bar.

Where do people with high cholesterol go for their holidays? Statin Island.

Nobody could have stopped Ashleigh and Pudsey winning *Britain's Got Talent* 2012. It was an act of dog.

Andy Murray stormed off court today after losing six straight games to a robot. When questioned afterwards, he said, 'It was a set up.'

I spent the last decade building a time machine. That's ten years of my life I will get back.

Did you hear about the guy who got his hand stuck up his backside? He said he felt fine in himself.

Teacher: Who can tell me what an arms race is?
Pupil: Is it another name for a wheelbarrow race, sir?

Today I taught my two-year-old daughter how

to say 'atop', 'aboard', 'skyward' and 'rising'. On words and up words.

My great grandparents died of consumption. They were eaten by a shark.

Pupils at Eton College have been picking on smaller kids by throwing bars of gold at them. The teachers have now launched an anti-bullion campaign.

Why was the crash mat worried? He knew he was for the high jump.

My uncle runs a business selling sandwiches with no fillings. It's his bread and butter.

I wonder if people with OCD are bothered by the fact that the D stands for disorder.

Death. It's all gravey.

What did the pastry chef do when he was released from prison? He made a fresh tart.

I had sex in a garden centre once. It was a bit seedy.

During the war, my grandfather suffered a neck injury. The doctor told him he had to keep it in a neutral position, so he moved to Switzerland.

Predictive text is getting frighteningly clever. I

was writing a text to this girl to ask her on a date, and the phone changed it to 'Don't bother; she thinks you're a moron.'

Why did the old man avoid eating sprouts before tending to his plants? He wanted to reduce his greenhouse gas emissions.

E.T. He was a light-hearted chap.

Did you hear about the IT geek who attached women to his computer? He had a girl in every port.

I tried watching *Black Swan* the other night. I sat there thinking, 'Blimey, this is the darkest film I've ever seen.' Then I realised I hadn't turned the TV on.

I once performed a phlebotomy on a Mick Jagger lookalike. It was like getting blood out of a Stone.

I took a bag of old calculators and abacuses to the charity shop. It wasn't worth much, but it all adds up.

I had a problem with my car so I took it to a garage and asked for a quote. The mechanic said, 'We are all in the gutter, but some of us are looking at the stars.'

THE END

NICK JONES

THANKS!

Thank you for reading this book. I really hope you enjoyed it!

For the latest news on the author please visit gaggedandbound.net or follow @nickjonezy on Twitter.

By the same author:

Gagged and Bound – a book of puns, one-liners and dad jokes

'It's what it says on the tin: a succession of one-liners, puns and dad jokes going at your laughing muscles in a joyously pell-mell, headlong way. It's irresistible.' **The Bookbag**

'This is a very funny book.' **Red City Review**

'I would recommend this book to anyone looking for a joke book that's varied and full of easy one-liners.' **Reader's Favorite**

Available in paperback and digital formats on Amazon and other websites.

Made in the USA
Charleston, SC
15 July 2015

gagged & bound 2

Following the success of his first book, the Amazo
bestseller *Gagged and Bound*, pun-loving gag writ
and self-proclaimed "sit-down comedian" Nick Jon
returns with another collection of original one-line
puns and dad jokes engineered to make you chuck
Packed with razor-sharp wordplay, downright sillines
and hilarious illustrations by Tiffany Sheely, *Gagg
and Bound 2* is bound to make you laugh!

Jokes include:

My dad had his nostril hair removed using electrolysis. The
results were great, but they charged him through the nose

I surprised my wife today by buying her a new pair of high
heels. I like to keep her on her toes.

A man was due in court today for stealing an invisibility cloa
He didn't show up.

I made a mountain out of a molehill earlier. It's a lot harder
than people say it is.

ISBN 9780993079412
90‹
9 780993 079412

RUM PRESS

what the..."

Conversation about Living

Darryl Bailey